What's the
BIG DEAL?
Why God Cares About Sex

Stan & Brenna Jones

NAVPRESS®
Bringing Truth to Life

OUR GUARANTEE TO YOU

We believe so strongly in the message of our books that we are making this quality guarantee to you. If for any reason you are disappointed with the content of this book, return the title page to us with your name and address and we will refund to you the list price of the book. To help us serve you better, please briefly describe why you were disappointed. Mail your refund request to: NavPress, P.O. Box 35002, Colorado Springs, CO 80935.

The Navigators is an international Christian organization. Our mission is to reach, disciple, and equip people to know Christ and to make Him known through successive generations. We envision multitudes of diverse people in the United States and every other nation who have a passionate love for Christ, live a lifestyle of sharing Christ's love, and multiply spiritual laborers among those without Christ.

NavPress is the publishing ministry of The Navigators. NavPress publications help believers learn biblical truth and apply what they learn to their lives and ministries. Our mission is to stimulate spiritual formation among our readers.

FOR A FREE CATALOG OF
NAVPRESS BOOKS & BIBLE STUDIES,
CALL 1-800-366-7788 (USA)
OR 1-800-839-4769 (CANADA)

CONTENTS

▼

To Brandon

ACKNOWLEDGMENTS

▼

We wish to thank the editorial, production, and marketing staff of NavPress, especially Steve Webb, for their support of this project. Cathy Davis provided immensely valuable feedback as our consulting children's editor; *What's the Big Deal?* and *Facing the Facts* especially benefited from her insights and editing skills. Our thanks go out to Sanna Baker and Carolyn Nystrom for reading and commenting on the early drafts of *The Story of Me*, and to Lisa, Mark, and Anna McMinn for reading and commenting on the early drafts of *What's the Big Deal?* Finally, our thanks to Carol Blauwkamp for help with typing parts of the early drafts of several of these books.

"GOD'S DESIGN FOR SEX" CHILDREN'S BOOK SERIES

▼

This book is one of a series designed to help parents shape their children's character, particularly in the area of sexuality. From their earliest years, our children are bombarded constantly with destructive and false messages about the nature of sexuality and the place of sexual intimacy in life through the media, discussions with their friends, and school sex-education programs. The result? Skyrocketing rates of teen sexual activity, pregnancy, abortion, sexually transmitted diseases, divorce, and devastated lives.

Our conclusion from studying this crisis, the nature of human sexuality, and most importantly, the Scriptures is that our God wants Christian parents to be the primary sex educators of their children. And if we are going to have a powerful impact, we must start early, working to lay a godly foundation of understanding of their sexuality before the twisted ideas of the world have a chance to take root. First messages are the most powerful; why wait until your child hears the wrong thing and then try to correct the misunderstanding? God made sexuality, and He made it as a beautiful gift; why not present it to our children the way God intended?

Our first book, *How and When to Tell Your Kids About Sex: A Lifelong Approach to Shaping Your Child's Sexual Character* (NavPress, 1993), was designed to provide parents with a comprehensive understanding of what they can do to shape their child's "sexual character." Some of our specific goals in that book were to:

- ☞ help you understand your role in shaping your child's views, attitudes, and beliefs about sexuality;
- ☞ help you understand and shape the building blocks of your child's character;
- ☞ clarify what God's view of our sexuality is;
- ☞ discuss how to explain and defend the traditional Christian view of sexual morality in these modern times;
- ☞ explore how you can most powerfully influence your child to make a decision for sexual abstinence (chastity); and
- ☞ equip you, the parent, to provide your child with the strengths necessary to stand by his or her commitments to traditional Christian morality.

In *How and When to Tell Your Kids About Sex* we provided numerous dialogues between parents and children at different ages, and offered many suggestions about how difficult subjects could be approached. Nevertheless, the most frequent comment we heard from parents who read our book was, "I really think you are right, but I don't think I can talk to my child that way. I wish there was something we could read with our children to get us started in discussing these matters." The books in this series are designed to meet that need.

For the sake of this children's book series, we have divided the years between birth and puberty into four time periods. We have made these periods overlap because there are differences in children's maturity levels that only you as a parent can know;

there are eight-year-olds who are more mature than some ten-year-olds, for example. The broad age ranges we have used are: three to five, five to eight, eight to eleven, and eleven to fourteen. We have written one book for each age range.

The first three of these four books are designed to be read *by parents to their children.* They are not, by themselves, meant to provide all of the information that kids need. They are to be *starting points* for you, the Christian parent, to discuss sexuality with your children in a manner appropriate to each age. They provide an anchor point for discussions, a jump-start to get discussions going. We suggest that you not simply hand these books to your child to read, because *it is how you as a parent handle the issue of sexuality that will have the greatest impact upon your child.* The fourth book is designed to be read by the child, now eleven to fourteen years in age, but we hope parents will also read the book and discuss its contents with the child.

Book One (Ages Three to Five): *The Story of Me*
Our most important task with a young child is to lay a spiritual *foundation* for the child's understanding of his or her sexuality. Book one helps you do that. It is vital that our children see their bodies and their sexuality (their "girl-ness" or "boy-ness") for what it is: a gift from God, a *marvelous* gift. They must see that God made their bodies on purpose, that God loves the human body (and the whole human person), and that God regards it as a work of divine art that in the beginning He called "very good" (Genesis 1:31). They must see that God loves women and men evenly; both are created in the image of God. Children must see not only their bodies, not only their existence as boys or girls, but also their sexual organs as a gift from God. They can begin to develop an appreciation for God's marvelous gift by understanding some of the basics of human reproduction, and so the growth of a child inside a mother's body and the birth process are discussed in this book. It is critical that children at this age begin to develop a trust for God's Law and see God as a law-

giver who has the best interests of His people at heart. Finally, it is critical at this stage that children come to see families as God's intended framework for the nurture and love of children. We hope you will find *The Story of Me* a wonderful starting point for discussing sexuality with your young child.

Book Two (Ages Five to Eight): *Before I Was Born* **(by Carolyn Nystrom)**

Building upon the topics in book one, Carolyn Nystrom further emphasizes the creational goodness of our bodies, our existence as men and women, and our sexual organs. New topics are introduced as well. The book discusses growth and change in a boy's body as he becomes a man, and in a girl's body as she becomes a woman. Tactfully and directly, it explains the basic nature of sexual intercourse between a husband and wife. Undergirding this information is the foundation of Christian morality: that God wants sexual intercourse limited to marriage because it brings a husband and wife together in a way that honors God and helps build strong families. This foundation will be vitally important later in the life of your child.

It is not uncommon for parents to ask, "Do my kids really need to know about sexual intercourse this early?" The answer is yes. First, there is no good rationale for keeping kids ignorant about this basic area of life. We must remember that the Hebrew people, in and through whom God revealed His divine will, were farmers and ranchers among whom the breeding of animals was part of everyday life. Further, their culture was one with much less privacy than we have today. Homes were small, without glass for windows or stereos for background noise, and three or more generations commonly lived together. It was in the context of a society steeped in what we politely call "animal husbandry," a society with little privacy and definite "earthy" attitudes toward sexuality, that our Lord's will and rules about sexuality were revealed. We don't need to shelter our kids by keeping them "in the dark."

The second reason for telling your kids about sexual intercourse early is that positive, first messages are always the most powerful. Our children are exposed to the facts about sexual intercourse on the playgrounds of their schools and in the backyards of our neighborhoods. If we want to shape godly attitudes in our children about sex, why would we wait until they soak in the errors and misperceptions of the world and then try to change their attitudes? Why not instead build from the foundation up?

Book Three (Ages Eight to Eleven): *What's the Big Deal? Why God Cares About Sex*

This book attempts to do three things. First, it attempts to review and reinforce the messages of the first two books: the basics of sexual intercourse and the fundamental creational goodness of our sexuality.

Second, it attempts to continue the task of explicitly and deliberately building your child's understanding of why God intends sexual intercourse to be reserved for marriage.

Third, this book will attempt to help you begin the process of "inoculating" your child against the negative moral messages of the world. In *How and When to Tell Your Kids About Sex* we argue that Christian parents should *not* try to shelter their children from all of the destructive moral messages of the secular world. When we shelter them, we leave them naive and vulnerable, and we risk communicating that these negative messages are so powerful that Christians cannot deal with them. Too much sheltering will leave our children defenseless against the attacks they will receive from the world.

But neither should we just let our kids be inundated with destructive messages. The principle of inoculation suggests that we gently expose our kids to the contrary moral messages they will soon hear anyway. It should be in our *homes* that our kids first learn that many people in our world do not believe in reserving sex for marriage, as well as getting their first understanding of such problems as teenage pregnancy, AIDS, and so forth. But they should be exposed to these realities *for a vital purpose*, so that we parents can help build their defenses against these terrible problems of our culture. In doing so, we can strengthen their resolve to stand by the traditional Christian ethic and send them into the world prepared to defend their beliefs and choices.

Book Four (Ages Eleven to Fourteen): *Facing the Facts: The Truth About Sex and You*

Facing the Facts: The Truth About Sex and You will attempt again to build upon all that has come before, but will prepare your child for puberty in more depth. Your child is now old enough for more detailed information about the changes her or his body is about to go through, and about the adult body that is soon to be presented to her or him as a gift from God. Your child also needs to be reminded about God's view of sexuality, about His loving and beautiful intentions for how this gift should be used. The distorted ways in which our world views sex must be clearly labeled, and our children must be prepared to face views and beliefs contrary to those we are teaching them at home. We attempt to do all this while also talking about the many confusing feelings of puberty and early adolescence. We hope that our talking about these feelings will encourage loving conversation between you and your developing children as they go through this challenging period. This book is meant to be read by the child himself or herself, but we urge you to read it too, and then talk about it with your child.

All of these books were written as if dialogue were an ongoing reality between a child, his or her mother and father, and other siblings in the home. Yet in some homes only one parent is willing to talk about sex; in others only one of two parents is a Christian. Many Christian parents are not in intact, two-parent, "traditional" homes. We hope these books will be used by and be useful to single parents, grandparents who are the primary care-givers to a child or children, parents with just one child, adoptive or foster parents, and other families that do not fit the "traditional" mold. Obviously, use of these books by "nontra-ditional" families will require some special creativity and thought. But this is really no different from the challenges you face in talking about sex with your child in the first place. Sex educa-tion is hard when you do not have a partner who can share the other gender's perspective, when an absent partner is not a good role model, or when discussion of the topic raises painful memories and unresolved issues. We are concerned about these challenges but urge you *to press onward anyway.* The wel-fare of your child requires that you address the issues raised in these books. Better that they be addressed constructively and directly than left to fester unexplored.

Thank you for trusting us to help you in this great adven-ture of shaping your child's sexual character. We hope these books will be valuable tools in raising a new generation of faith-ful Christian young people who will have healthy, positive, accept-ing attitudes about their own sexuality; who will live confi-dent, chaste lives as faithful witnesses to the work of Christ in their lives while they are single, and then fulfilled, loving, reward-ing lives as spouses.

Remember that what you tell your child about sexuality is only part of the puzzle. How you live your lives as parents before your children will have the greatest impact upon them. Teenagers who have a close relationship with a parent are better prepared to resist sexual temptation and pressure than those who are dis-connected from their parents; work on having a loving, caring, listening, supportive relationship with your teens. Encourage their own unique, independent relationship with the living God by family church attendance, by prayer and study of the Scriptures individually and as a family, and by the ways in which you live your everyday lives (Deuteronomy 6:1-9). Prayerfully send them out into the world, and always be available as a model of God's love, discipline, and forgiveness.

CHAPTER ONE

WHAT'S THE BIG DEAL?

▼

SAM: Dad, what's the big deal about sex? Why do people talk so much about sex, like on TV and stuff? Why do the big kids joke about it, and why do grownup people seem to think about it so much?

DAD: Well, you won't understand some of that until you are a grownup. But I will try to explain it as best I can. First, remember that we've said that sex is a wonderful gift from God. God did a marvelous thing making men and women, girls and boys, different from each other. Our bodies are a gift from God. When husbands and wives share their bodies together in sexual intercourse, that is part of the way they share their love with each other. It is only one of the ways, but it is an important and wonderful way. So, one reason why sex is such a big deal is because sex is a marvelous gift from God.

17

AMY: But I don't hear people talking about sex a lot because it is a gift from God!

DAD: You got me there! I'm glad you are thinking about this enough to see that! I guess what I meant was that sex is important in everyone's life because God made us that way: He made us men and women with special bodies, and he made adults so that they are interested in sex. And he made sexual intercourse a special gift for husbands and wives.

But you know what? That's not really why sex is such a big thing today. Most of the reasons people have for making sex such a big deal are bad reasons, not good ones. For instance, sex is a big deal because of all the pain and suffering that happen when people don't use God's gift rightly. Sex becomes a big deal because people want to talk about the bad things that happen because of sex. When people use the gift of sex the way God meant it to be used, it is much more likely to have a beautiful and wonderful result.

 SAM: What kinds of bad things?

MOM: Here's one example. Whenever a couple has sexual intercourse, there is a chance of the woman getting pregnant, of getting a baby in her womb. If the man and woman are married, this is usually a happy time when they feel like celebrating. But if the woman who has sex and gets pregnant is a fourteen-year-old girl, she is usually not happy. She may have to raise a baby without a husband. Her whole life changes—her dreams about finishing high school, dating, going to college, everything. God meant for pregnancy and giving birth to a child to be wonderful, something worth really celebrating. But having a baby is something that many people dread because they didn't save sex for marriage.

DAD: Misusing God's gift of sex also spreads some diseases. Did you know that if a man and a woman never have sex with anyone except each other when they get married, those two people have almost no chance of ever getting any diseases from sex at all? But because so many young people today are not waiting to get married before they have sex, there are terrible diseases that are becoming more common. One of these is the disease called AIDS, and we can talk about that another time.

When sex is treated like a beautiful gift and used the way God wants us to use it, sex really is a beautiful gift. If you use God's gift correctly, you can be wonderfully happy that God made you a boy or a girl. But when sex is misused, it almost always hurts people. That is one major reason why people today make such a big deal about sex—because so many people are being hurt by sex. Did you know that almost one million teenage girls get pregnant every year? Did you know that more and more teenagers are getting sexual diseases because they do not follow God's rules?

MOM: Another reason sex is a big deal is because the world makes it more important than it should be. Do you remember what the Bible says about idolatry? People commit idolatry when they take something that God has made and then treat it like it is a god. In the Old Testament, God hated it when people took things He had made, like rocks and trees and gold, and then worshiped those things. Someone once said that when people stop believing in the real God, they start believing that other things can take God's place.

Many things take the place of God in people's lives today—like money, or power, or being famous. Sex is sort of like a god for some people today. They think that sex will make them happy. But only God can make us truly happy. So when they try to get happy by having as much

sex as possible or by breaking God's rules about sex, they usually find they are not happy at all.

 AMY: I think I understand that, but is that why people joke about sex so much?

 DAD: I think that's part of the reason. This is a terrible problem with TV and movies today. In a lot of television shows and movies, people talk about sex, joke about sex, think about sex all the time. I worry that these shows teach kids and grownups that sex is worth thinking about all the time. We Christians think sex is a wonderful gift. But it was not meant to take the place of God in our lives. And thinking about sex all the time or making sex the most important thing in our lives can never make us happy.

SAM: But why do kids joke about sex so much?

MOM: I think it's because they hear how adults, especially on TV and in the movies, talk about it a lot, but the kids don't really know for sure what the adults are talking about. So the kids are really curious about it. Also—and I hope this isn't true for you two—many kids can't talk openly with their parents about sex. So they joke about it because they don't really understand it. They especially don't understand how God made it special, and they can't just talk normally with their parents about it because they are embarrassed about sex.

DAD: But now let me tell you why I think sex needs to be a big deal for us. We want to teach you the truth about sex so that you will be ready to make the right decisions about it as a teenager and adult. Please always feel free to ask us any questions that come to your mind, because we won't be able to think of everything you need to know. And we won't always know the answers to your questions! We might need to think about it a while before we answer you, but that's okay. It is important for us to keep talking about this topic. We love you so much that we want you to learn about how God made us and meant for us to live, even when it isn't always easy to talk about.

Some Questions to Discuss
1. When have you heard kids joke about sex? Why do you think they do that?
2. What have you noticed about the way television and movies talk about sex?
3. What do you think about God making you a sexual person?

CHAPTER TWO

WHY DO PEOPLE DO THAT?

▼

SAM: Dad, did you really mean it when you said I could ask you anything about sex?

DAD: Yes, son, I really did mean it. Sex is a gift from God, and I want you to understand that gift. So I want you to ask me any question you might have.

SAM: Well, I have a question. You and Mom told me that sexual intercourse is when a man puts his penis inside a woman's vagina. And I know that's how a baby gets made.

DAD: That's right.

SAM: But I thought people would only do that to have a baby. Do people have sex when they aren't trying to have a baby? Do you have a baby every time you have sex? Why would people have sex if they didn't want to have a baby?

DAD: Wow! Those are great questions! Let me try to answer the first two questions together. The answer to your first question is yes. People do have sex even when they are not trying to have a baby. I'll explain why in just a minute. The answer to your second question is no. People do not get pregnant with a baby every time they have sex. And here's why.

Remember how a man's body makes little tiny cells called sperm? One way of thinking of sperm is that they are like seeds. If we were to take a seed from this apple, plant it in the ground, and treat it right, it might grow into a tall apple tree. It doesn't need anything else to become a tree.

But a sperm is different from a real seed because it can't grow into a human being by itself. A sperm is really like half of a seed. To grow into a human being it has to join with the other half. That other half is the egg or ovum that is inside the woman's body. When a man has sexual intercourse with his wife millions and millions of sperm come out of his body all at once. Only a few drops of liquid come out when a man has sexual intercourse, but in those drops are usually over 200 million sperm. There are about as many sperm inside those few drops as there are people in the entire United States. So you can imagine how tiny sperm are.

When the sperm come out of a man's penis into the woman's vagina when they have sexual intercourse, some of the sperm begin to swim up into her womb. You remember how a woman's vagina connects inside her body to her uterus or womb? The sperm begin trying to swim up into her body to meet with an egg. Now, though a man's body makes millions and millions of sperm, most of the time a woman's body only releases one egg a month. That egg is only ready to meet with a sperm for about one day out of the month. So there are only a few days each month when a woman can get pregnant. If she has sexual intercourse any other day, she is not going to get pregnant. Most couples do not know for sure exactly when the woman can get pregnant.

The sperm joining with the egg is really an amazing event. Did that all make sense?

SAM: Yes, it made sense, but I still don't understand why people would have sex if they're not trying to have a baby.

DAD: Okay. This is a little bit harder to explain. Sexual intercourse is not just for making babies. The Bible says when a man and a woman have sexual intercourse they become "one flesh." See, here in the first book of the Bible it says, "Therefore a man leaves his father and his mother and clings to his wife, and they become one flesh. And the man and his wife were both naked, and were not ashamed" (Genesis 2:24-25). And in the New Testament, it says, "The two shall be one flesh" (1 Corinthians 6:16).

God wants your mom and me to love each other very much and stay married for all of our lives. He wants us to create a home of love that will be a good place for you and your brother and sister to grow up. He also wants other people to be able to look at us and think about how much God loves them, because our love is a good example of what real, faithful love is like. God gave sexual intercourse as a special gift that would help make this happen. Do you remember the verse I just read about the man and woman being naked and not being ashamed? Imagine that you were naked in front of somebody you hardly knew. How would you feel?

 SAM: That would feel embarrassing! I'd run away!

DAD: You probably would. But God wants people who get married to have such a special love for the person they marry that they don't have to hide anything from the other person, not even their private parts. And God made sexual intercourse as a special thing that a husband and wife can do together—something they don't do with anyone else. In that way, sexual intercourse becomes something that helps to glue a husband and wife together. I won't have sex with anyone but your mom, and your mom won't have sex with anyone but me. This is something special between the two of us.

 SAM: So is that it? Is that the reason people have sex?

 DAD: No, there's something else. God made sex so that it feels really good for both the man and the woman. Every man's penis is very sensitive. When a husband and wife have sexual intercourse, the feeling of his penis being in his wife's vagina is wonderful to him. And it feels wonderful for the woman as well, because God made her vagina and the area around her vagina to be very sensitive, just like the man's penis. Not only that, but God made a little spot just above the opening of the vagina that is called the clitoris. This little place on the woman's body is there only to give her pleasure from sex with her husband.

So sexual intercourse makes a husband and wife feel really good, and that helps them to love each other more and more, because they are able to please each other and give each other great joy. Having sexual intercourse strengthens their love and draws them close together. This is why many people call sexual intercourse "making love." If making love is loving and gentle and good, it helps the wife and husband love each other more.

 SAM: So do you and Mom have sex even when you aren't trying to have a baby? How much do you do it?

DAD: Yes, we do. But I don't want to tell you exactly how often we make love or when. That is a private matter between your mom and me. Some couples make love once or twice a week, while others enjoy making love more often, maybe four or five times a week, and some are happy doing it less often.

When people who aren't married have sexual intercourse, they have reasons for having sex, too, but they aren't good reasons. Let's talk about those reasons another time. But I am very thankful that your mom and I can have sexual intercourse together; it makes our love for each other stronger. Even when we are not trying to have a baby, having sexual intercourse is a wonderful way for me to say that I love your mom in a special way that I don't love anyone else. It helps us be united together. And it feels good. Those are some of the reasons we have sex when we aren't trying to have a baby. They're good reasons that make God happy. I'm thankful that God gave us this gift in our marriage.

Some Questions to Discuss

1. What do some other kids you know say about why people have sex?
2. What are the reasons God made sex?

CHAPTER THREE

SEX OUTSIDE OF MARRIAGE

▼

AMY: Mom, you know how you have always told us that sex is something that should only happen in marriage? You've always said that God only wants girls to have sex with their husbands and boys to have sex with their wives. If that's true, why does everybody talk about having sex with boyfriends and girlfriends and even people they just meet?

MOM: Yes, honey, I know what you mean. Is there somebody at school who is talking about that, or one of your friends here in the neighborhood?

AMY: No, I guess I just mean that on TV an awful lot of people talk about having sex when they aren't married. It seems like almost all the teenagers on TV wind up having sex.

MOM: Okay, that helps me know what you are thinking. I'll try to give you as honest an answer

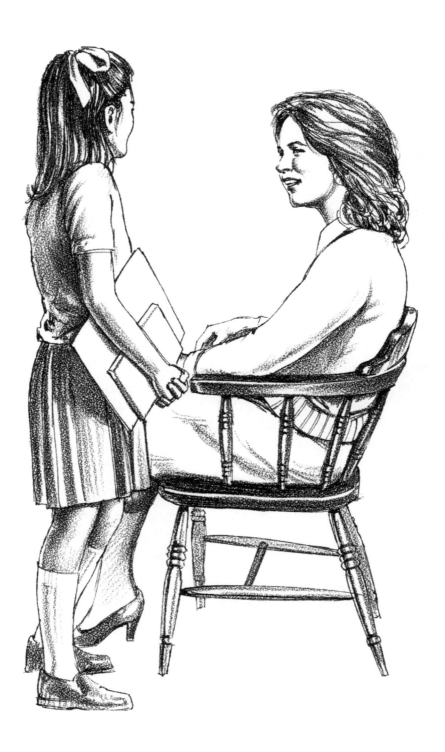

as I can. First, what is shown on TV is not real life. The people on TV, especially the teenagers, don't show what real life is like.

God gave this beautiful gift of sex with some instructions for how we should use it. Dad just bought a new lawn mower. If Dad were to ignore the instructions that came with the lawn mower and try to use it for cutting sticks and wood instead of grass, he would very quickly find himself with a broken lawn mower. A broken mower will no longer do what a lawn mower was designed to do, which is to cut grass.

God's gift of sex is like that. God's gift of sexual intercourse was meant to help a man and a woman stay married to each other all their lives and feel very close and in love. When people have sex outside of marriage, they are not following God's instructions, and that means trouble.

 AMY: But why would they do it, then?

MOM: For a number of reasons. First, people have sex outside of marriage because sex makes their bodies feel good. Sometimes that makes them happy for a little while. But some things that feel good are not good to do. When you are mad, it might feel good to hit or hurt another person. But that doesn't make it right. The reason people take drugs is because the drugs make them feel good. But taking drugs destroys your life rather than making it better. It tastes good to stuff yourself with your favorite candy, but that could make you sick.

A lot of kids who have sex because it feels good do that because their lives are kind of empty. They are confused about why they are living at all. Many of the kids you know at school probably think that the only reason for living is to have as much fun and as many good times as they can have. They don't think about their own life having a more important meaning. Isn't it sad that they don't know how much God loves them and that God made them to have a wonderful life being His son or daughter and living the way that is best for them? Many kids today think their lives have no meaning at all. When they get to be teenagers, they may think that having sex is just one more way to have as much fun as they can.

Another reason why people who are not married have sex is that they use sex as a way of showing that they like or care for someone. In fact, I think this is one of the most common reasons. People often talk about sex as a way of showing love. Many people call sex "making love." Sexual intercourse between a husband and a wife really is a way of "making love." Married couples have sex with one another because they love each other. Sex helps them to be closer and love each other more.

But sex between two people who are not married isn't really "making love." Most people who have sex when they aren't married don't really love each other. They may like each other and get excited about each other, but real love is something that grows over time, and real love means they promise to stay together for all of their lives.

People have sex for lots of other reasons as well. One of the worst reasons is because their friends pressure them to. It won't be too long before you are in middle school, and soon after that you will be in high school. You will soon hear people saying you are not a real woman if you don't have sex. That there is something wrong with you if you don't have sex. That you are a prude if you don't have sex. That you have to prove that you deserve to be with the popular group by having sex.

Some kids can't stand it if other kids don't think they're cool. Some kids are so lonely or so confused that they will do whatever other kids are doing just so they won't be different. You don't have to prove anything to anyone by having sex.

You can see that there are no good reasons for having sex before marriage. Even so, by the time they leave high school, most teenagers have had sex at least one time, and many will choose to have sex often. You will need to be very strong and know exactly what you believe if you are going to live the best way, the way God wants you to.

Some Questions to Discuss
1. What are some bad reasons for having sex?
2. Can you think of some times when other kids around you tried to get you to do something you knew was wrong, that you weren't supposed to do?
3. How can you stay strong to do what is right when others want you to do what is wrong?

CHAPTER FOUR

WHAT DOES GOD REALLY SAY ABOUT IT?

▼

Dear Amy and Sam,

You two have asked some good questions lately about your bodies and about sex. We know that one of the scariest things about becoming an adult is that you will begin choosing more and more what you really believe and make decisions that will change the rest of your life. For the rest of your lives, people will be telling you all sorts of different things about what is right, what will make you happy, and how you should live. You will have to choose who you believe as you make these important decisions, because not everyone can be right!

We are trying to teach you God's ways, and the Bible is where we can learn about God's ways. Here are some verses from the Bible for you to read. We have written them down, along with some things for you to think about as you try to understand what these verses mean. Why don't you look up these verses in your Bibles? If you want, you can mark them so they will always be easy to find, because they are very important. Happy hunting!

After you read these verses, we can talk about any questions you might have.

Love,
Mom and Dad

P.S. After the verses and our comments, we wrote down three reasons for saving sexual intercourse for marriage. Hope these ideas make sense to you.

Proverbs 3:5-6 (**hint:** this is about in the middle of the Bible, in the Old Testament) says,

Trust in the LORD with all your heart,
  and do not rely on your own insight.
In all your ways acknowledge him,
  and He will make straight your paths.

This means that our own insights or ideas, and the ideas of people around us, can lead us the wrong way. But God's truth is like a perfect map that will always guide us on a good, straight road. God's truth will help us live our lives in the way that's best for us, that will make us the happiest we can ever hope to be. So if God's truth is the best guide for our lives, then we should ask what God says about whom we should have sex with. God says in the Bible that only people who are married to each other should have sex.

First Corinthians 6:13,18-20 (**hint:** this is in the New Testament) says, "The body is meant not for fornication but for the Lord, and the Lord for the body. . . . Shun fornication! Every sin that a person commits is outside the body; but the fornicator sins against the body itself. Or do you not know that your body is a temple of the Holy Spirit within you, which you have from God, and that you are not your own? For you were bought with a price; therefore glorify God in your body."

In the Bible, the word **fornication** means sex with anyone other than your husband or wife. God doesn't just say "don't do it"; instead He says, "Shun it!" That means you should stay away from it like it was a deadly disease. Other Bible translations say we should "flee" fornication—run away from it as if you were running away from a robber or a fire! How important do you think it must be to God for us not to have sex before marriage if we should shun it or flee from it? And isn't it interesting that we can glorify God by what we do with our bodies?

First Thessalonians 4:3-5,7 (**hint:** this book is five short books after 1 Corinthians) says, "For this is the will of God, your sanctification: that you abstain from fornication; that each one of you know how to control your own body in holiness and honor, not with lustful passion, like the Gentiles who do not know God. . . . For God did not call us to impurity but in holiness."

This verse and the 1 Corinthians verse are only two of the many places in the Bible where God says sex outside of marriage is wrong. **Sanctification** is a big word that means "cleaning up" or "purifying," so this verse teaches that God wants us to clean the evil out of our lives, and one important evil He wants cleaned out is sexual immorality.

Hebrews 13:4 (a few books after 1 Thessalonians) says, "Let marriage be held in honor by all, and let the marriage bed be kept undefiled; for God will judge fornicators and adulterers."

"Marriage bed" is a polite way of talking about sex between the husband and wife, which is one of the things (besides sleeping and talking and just hugging) that people do in their marriage bed. This is one of the many places in the Bible that says God's gift of sex between a wife and husband is special and meant only for the two of them. When husbands and wives use God's gift of sex the way God wants them to, they are keeping God's gift pure. And that will make them happy, and God too!

Writing these verses down helped us see that there are three main reasons not to have sex with anyone but your husband or wife.

1. We should save sex for marriage because God has told us that is what sex is truly made for. Many people today think that sex is just made for fun or to prove you are grown up. But God says sexual intercourse was created to help make a wife and a husband, two separate people, become "one flesh," to glue them together for life and help them have a better and more loving marriage. A husband and wife have the special joy of having one special person they can be close to, glued to, for all of life. Sex with your husband or wife can be part of the glue that helps to hold you together.

2. We should follow God's rules because He wants us to. Obeying those rules is a way of showing God that we love Him. Jesus said, "If you love me, you will keep my commandments. . . . Those who love me will keep my word" (John 14:15,23). If you said you loved us, but you never obeyed us, we would have a hard time believing that you really did love us. One way we show who we love is by who we obey. God wants us to love and trust Him enough that we obey Him.

3. We should save sex for marriage because God's plan is the best plan for our lives. It is the way that will bring us the most happiness. People who break God's rules take big chances that they may hurt themselves badly by getting pregnant when they shouldn't, by catching diseases, and by being less able to have a good marriage. When we follow God's rules, we are protecting ourselves from harm and preparing ourselves to enjoy the good things God wants to give us in our lives.

Those are three good reasons to follow God's ways!

Some Questions to Discuss

1. How is God's Word, the Bible, like a map for our lives?
2. What does the Bible say about having sex with someone other than your husband or wife?

CHAPTER FIVE

THE CHANGES OF PUBERTY

▼

 AMY: Mom, there's something that I just don't get. I don't really like boys that much. How come girls start liking boys so much when I don't feel anything like that now?

MOM: You know, I remember feeling just like you do. I remember in third and fourth grades thinking that kissing a boy would be really awful. I remember wondering why my older brother and sister seemed to be so crazy about dating. I especially remember when my older sister would be sure that she was in love with some boy. She would write his name over and over again and wait by the phone for him to call. I just didn't get it! Why was she so crazy about boys?

 AMY: That is exactly what I mean. I don't get it.

41

MOM: It's still a real mystery to me, too, why it happens. But I'll tell you something: It's a wonderful thing that both young men and young women can feel that another person is so very special. God made us that way! It's probably good that we don't experience those same feelings when we are children. We have to get to a certain point in growing up before we feel that way.

One of the most marvelous feelings you will ever have is what people call "falling in love." I know it doesn't sound that good right now; I can even see when I talk about it now that you wrinkle up your nose like you can't stand the thought! But someday you will be glad that this happens to you.

 AMY: Well, I'm not glad yet!

MOM: But you will be! God made us so that as we grow up, we don't want to be alone. Instead, we want to have a special someone we can share the rest of our lives with.

Dad and I love you very much, and when you were a baby, our love was about all you needed. But after a while, you still wanted our love but also wanted to have friends too. And there will come a point, when you become a young woman, when the love of your mom and dad, and even of friends, won't be enough anymore. You will feel a desire to love someone special. In fact, you will feel ready to fall in love.

I think God gave us this gift for a lot of different reasons. Being able to fall in love makes it possible to have one of the greatest gifts that God can ever give—a good marriage. For a good marriage to work, it has to be filled with love. A loving marriage may give you the chance to have children and to pass your love on to them. And being able to fall in love reminds every one of us that we were not made to be alone. It is like a reminder every day of our need for God. Even if you don't get married, these feelings are still a big part of being a grownup.

 AMY: But how does it happen? How do your feelings change so much?

 MOM: Part of the change happens in our hearts and minds and feelings, and part of it occurs in our bodies. The part that's in our hearts and minds and feelings happens when you are ready to be an adult and to have a special person to share your life with. You don't want to be taken care of like a child anymore. Instead, you feel ready to get out more on your own and really live your own life. But I'll tell you a secret: Being an adult can be a bit lonely and frightening sometimes. It's an awfully big and scary world out there. But God loves us and wants to comfort us. Trusting Him helps us not to be frightened of all the things that can happen in our world. It's also a gift from God when we can share our adult life with another person who is our partner.

You have already started to become an adult, though you are a ways away yet. When your feelings begin to change, and you begin to think, *Maybe it wouldn't be so bad to like that boy*, you will know that you are beginning the wonderful transformation toward becoming a young woman. I am excited for you as you go through this, though it sure is a scary time full of ups and downs.

 AMY: What about our bodies? You said our bodies are part of the change.

 MOM: That's right! You've heard about puberty already. Puberty is a period of two, three, or four years when our bodies gradually change from being bodies of big kids to being bodies of developing adults. That's the time when we begin to grow more hair on our bodies, especially pubic hair right above our genitals. Puberty is the time when kids go through a real growth spurt and grow closer to the size they will eventually be as adults. It is the time when a boy's voice starts to change. Muscles begin to grow and the shape of your body starts to look more like an adult's. A young woman's breasts begin to develop, and she starts to wear a bra.

Puberty is also the time when your sexual organs begin to change in marvelous ways that make them physically ready for you to have sexual intercourse and to become a parent. For young men, this means that their bodies start to produce sperm that make them capable of becoming fathers. For young women, this means that the eggs in their ovaries mature and they begin to have their periods, which is a sure sign that their bodies are in the process of getting ready to become pregnant if they have sexual intercourse.

 AMY: What is it we do to make those changes start?

MOM: Nothing! You can't do anything to make the changes start earlier or later; they just happen. For some kids the changes start early, around age ten, and for others they happen later, at age fourteen or fifteen. What starts the whole puberty thing off, though, is that for some mysterious reason our brains begin to tell our bodies to produce sex hormones. A woman's most important sex hormones are produced in her ovaries inside her abdomen, where her eggs are stored. A young man's sex hormones are produced in his testes, which rest inside the muscle and skin sac, the scrotum, that is right underneath his penis. The testes are also where the boy's sperm are produced.

These hormones that are put out by the young man's testes and the young woman's ovaries are what cause all these marvelous changes in the body. These hormones also

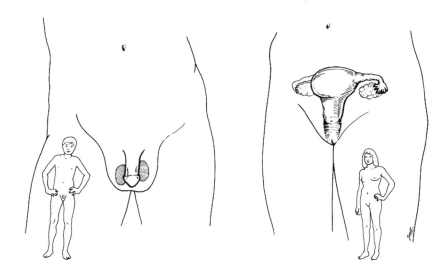

have an effect on our brains. I remember once when I told you about sexual intercourse, you said, "That is so gross. I can't believe that people do that." But after these hormones begin to circulate all through our bodies, even in our brains, the things that sounded gross once upon a time no longer sound so gross. In fact, they sound rather nice. These hormones don't make us have sex. But they do help us change so that it will begin to sound really nice for you to be close to a young man, or for a young man to be close to a young woman. Teenagers begin to have vague feelings that they just wish they could have sex, because the idea of it just sounds wonderful. They have these feelings even though they haven't ever had sex before and don't really know what it feels like at all.

 AMY: That must be really weird to change like that!

MOM: It is! When all of this begins to happen to you, it will feel rather strange. I remember feeling really mixed up about it all. Without knowing why, I went from thinking boys were stinky, to thinking they weren't so bad, to really hoping that one of them would like me because I sure did think he was wonderful. And for some reason I felt totally embarrassed about the way my feelings were changing.

Your dad tells me that he felt almost the same way. Boys go from thinking they can't stand girls to thinking they aren't so bad to thinking about falling in love and having sex a lot. Both boys and girls who are becoming men and women think about both love and sex a lot, but girls probably think more about the love part and boys more about the sex part when they are teenagers.

I hope you can keep talking to me about this. But if you are like me, this whole area will feel a little awful and embarrassing to talk about. That's okay—it makes it harder to talk, but it is perfectly normal to feel those feelings.

And remember: All this is happening because God is making you into something new, something you have never been before. He is changing you from being a child to being an adult. It doesn't always feel comfortable because God is not done with His changes. But you have to go through these changes to become the adult He wants you to be.

Some Questions to Discuss

1. What do you think about the way God made your body to change and grow? Does it sound scary, or exciting, or what?
2. What things about being an adult do you most look forward to?

CHAPTER SIX

BUT WHY CAN'T I DO THAT?

▼

SAM: Dad, you know how you won't let us watch movies or TV programs that have sex in them? Like R-rated movies?

DAD: Yes, it's very important to your mom and me that your sisters and you not see things like that. What are you thinking about that?

SAM: Some of the kids at school get to watch movies like that all the time. Their parents have cable television and don't really care what they watch. Some of the movies sound really cool.

DAD: Do you wish you could see those movies because everyone is talking about them?

SAM: Well, sort of. I don't want to watch anything that's dirty or bad, but some of the movies just sound really great the way the other kids describe them. I just don't understand.

DAD: I'm really glad you wanted to talk with me about it. I'll try to tell you what I think about this. Then, even though I'm not very likely to change my mind, I really want you to tell me what you think about what I've said.

Your mom and I have always tried to teach you what we believe is God's truth about sex. God made men and women different on purpose. When a man and a woman grow to love each other and choose to get married, their bodies are one part of the wonderful way God made them able to join together as husband and wife. A husband and wife are sharing their bodies completely when their bodies are fitted together by the man's penis being in the woman's vagina. Sharing their bodies should draw them closer to each other and help build their love. That is what we call sexual intercourse, and that's a gift to them from God.

Just having sexual intercourse doesn't make them perfectly close, however. If their marriage is going to be all that God intended, their hearts should be filled with love for one another. But sexual intercourse is special; God made it that way. The Bible teaches that when two people have sexual intercourse, their lives are joined together in some special way that we don't really understand. Your mom and I understand that we are strongly connected to each other, and part of that is because we have sexual intercourse with each other.

God thinks sexual intercourse is so special that He wants us to keep it only for marriage. God wants marriage to last as long as you live. It doesn't always work out that way. Lots of people are divorced. But God wants a man and woman to have a beautiful life together for as long as they live.

Some people break God's Law by having sex before they get married. They have sex with people they are not married to. Other people break God's Law even when they are married by having sex with someone other than their husband or wife. This makes God very sad. Sex is so special in God's eyes that He wants us to keep it only for the person we are married to.

 SAM: But what does this have to do with movies?

DAD: I'm taking a while to get there, aren't I? Okay. If that is God's thinking about sex, then what is being taught about sex in those movies your friends are watching? In fact, let's not just talk about movies, but let's talk about TV programs, advertisements in magazines, and posters that show women or men with hardly any clothes on or no clothes on at all. You may not know the word *pornography*, but you have probably heard of dirty magazines or dirty books that show photographs of people who are completely naked or show pictures of people having sex and things like that.

SAM: Yeah, one of the kids at school said he had found one of those magazines and that kids could look at it when they come over to his house. I didn't see it.

DAD: Well, I'm glad for that! Magazines, movies that show people naked or having sex—all of these things are saying something about sex. Suppose there is a movie that has lots of good chase scenes and car wrecks and so forth, but it also shows a man and a woman meeting for the first time, sort of liking each other even though they don't really know each other, and then they immediately start having sex. The people who made the movie make the two people look really beautiful, and they play just the right music and use just the right lights and show just the right things to make it seem very exciting. And then after they have sex it shows the two people (who are really just

actors) being all happy about what they did, and there are no problems whatsoever from what they chose to do. Now, what do you think something like that would teach a young person like you who is watching that movie?

 SAM: Well, I guess it would teach me that what those two people did was okay . . . maybe that it's something exciting to do?

 DAD: I think you are exactly right. We sometimes forget when we are watching a movie or a TV program that it's a completely made-up story. What we watch can really have an effect on us. If it's a fantasy movie where we are seeing nothing but weird creatures from Mars, we are probably not very affected by it. But almost every movie and television program today shows the same thing: people having sex when they've barely met. And it's always exciting and perfect.

After watching these things over and over, we might really begin to believe that sex between people who have just met is wonderful; that it is a good way to say "I like you" or "I love you"; that sex is always exciting; that people are never hurt, or given a disease, or get pregnant by having sex. We know this is a lie. Yet, if we watch such things all the time, we may find it harder to believe the truth.

Let me give you a different example. If a young boy spends a lot of time looking at pictures of naked women or women with few clothes on, what might that be teaching the boy? Or suppose a boy plasters his room with posters of nearly naked women; what is he learning?

 SAM: I don't know. That women's bodies are beautiful?

 DAD: Well, maybe, but most men already believe that women's bodies are beautiful. I think it's something different. I think boys begin to learn that it's okay to treat a woman like an object—like a thing. The women who posed for those pictures have basically let themselves be turned into things. I am worried that boys who spend all their time looking at pictures like that begin to think it is okay to treat all women like things because that is the way they are used to thinking about the women in those pictures.

I think it is also true that boys who look at such pictures all the time can begin to think that there is only one way for a woman to be beautiful, and that is to have exactly the kind of body that is shown in the pictures. Boys can begin to believe that women should show off their bodies like the pictures do. I think this is really ugly and destructive.

Women are not things; they are people. They need to be treated as people. A lot of people—even people who aren't Christians—agree that pornography and some commercials on TV or ads in magazines create a lot of trouble for women. They make men look at women just for their bodies rather than as real people to love and respect.

That is why I don't want you to see those movies or pictures. I'm trying to give you time to grow strong in believing the right way, God's way. You'll have plenty of chances to make your own decisions later in your life. The older you get, the more other people are going to try to get you to stop believing Christian truth and start thinking about sex in other ways.

Think of it this way. You are sort of like an athlete who is facing the biggest contest of your life just a few years from now. I am your coach who is trying to help you build up your strength and endurance for that big contest. I would be a very poor coach if I let you take on too much at this point in your training. If you try to lift weights that are too heavy for you, you can really hurt yourself. Maybe you will be able to handle those heavy weights later, but only if you work with lighter weights now. I want you to be ready for the big contest that is going to happen when you are a young adult. To give you the best chance to really be ready for that big contest, I am trying to protect you now from anything that would make you less strong later. What do you think about that?

Some Questions to Discuss
1. What are some ways in which the programs and movies we watch and the things we read can change how we think about sex, God, family, and other things?
2. How are people hurt by looking at "dirty" pictures?

CHAPTER SEVEN

WHAT IS AIDS?

▼

SAM: Mom, I saw a poster at the high school that said we could prevent AIDS with condoms, but I don't know what condoms are and I don't know what AIDS is. I know it's a bad disease because people seem to be afraid of it. But what is it?

MOM: I'll start with AIDS because that's a little bit easier to explain, and I'm awfully glad you asked me.

AIDS is a disease, a terrible disease, one of the few in our world that kills almost every person who gets the germ that causes it. That germ is called HIV, which are the initials of a very complicated label that describes what the germ does.

HIV is a particular type of germ called a virus. It gets into the cells of a person's body and stops that person's body from fighting diseases.

We have talked before about how your body is a miracle in its ability to fight off disease. When your body is

55

healthy, it senses germs that might cause you to come down with various diseases and figures out a unique way to fight each of those germs. This is how your body manages to stay healthy. HIV, though, begins to destroy the ability your body has to fight off disease. When a person is very sick from the HIV virus that person is described as having AIDS. People don't really die of the HIV virus. Rather, they die from another disease that their body could have protected them against if HIV had not wrecked their ability to fight off that disease.

 SAM: That sounds horrible! What if I get AIDS?

MOM: I hope you never do. The wonderful thing is that there are some specific things you can do to not get the HIV infection. But to explain this, I have to explain how AIDS is spread. There are lots of wild stories about this, but scientists are pretty sure they understand the real way it spreads. For some reason, there are more of the HIV germs in the blood of a person who has the HIV infection, and in the semen that comes out of the man's penis when he has sex, than in any other area of the person's body.

Almost all the people who have the HIV virus got it from doing one of two things: Either they took drugs from a needle that had the HIV-virus germs on it, or else they had sex with someone who had the virus and got it from that person. But not everyone gets the HIV infection this way. A few children have been given the virus because their mothers had it when they were pregnant and the mother, without meaning to, passed it to her baby through her own blood. A few other people got infected by having operations where they were given blood that had HIV in it before doctors knew how to make sure the blood was clean from HIV.

Most people who have AIDS got the HIV virus because they did things that broke God's rules. Some people chose to use drugs even though they shouldn't. The people who get HIV by taking drugs get it because they sometimes want drugs so much that they shoot the drugs into their bodies with a needle that someone else has also used for drugs. If the first person had the HIV virus, then the tiniest drops of blood on that needle can carry the virus from the first person to the second.

Some people choose to have sex with people they are not married to, even though they shouldn't. If a man has the HIV virus, then he can give it to a woman he has sex with because the virus is in his semen that comes out of his penis. Then that woman can give the virus to another man if she has sex with someone else later on. Some people have sex with lots of other people. The more people someone has sex with, the more likely it is that they will catch the HIV virus. This is why so many homosexual men have the HIV virus and have died. Many homosexual men like to have sex with lots of different people, even strangers they do not know.

But I want to tell you something important. These people broke God's rules, and because they did, they made it more likely that they would get the HIV virus. But that does not mean God gave them the virus and that God is punishing them for being bad. In the Bible, there are some places where God tells His people through His special messengers, the prophets, that He is sending a sickness on the people as a punishment for them doing bad things. Today, some speakers say that the spreading HIV disease is just like that. But I do not agree, because I think that only a prophet who speaks for God can say that kind of thing for sure.

People who use drugs and break God's rules about sex are doing bad things. But we all do bad things—you and I, your dad, everyone in our family, in our church, and everywhere. We all deserve to be punished by God. We should try not to do the bad things those people who have HIV did, but we should not pretend that we are better than them. And we must not hate them or say we are happy they are dying for the bad things they did. They did bad things, just as we do bad things. We should love them the way we would want to be loved.

HIV and AIDS is one more reason why it is so important to follow God's rules about sex. Any couple who lives the way God wants them to—not having sex until they are married and only having sex with the person they married—that couple is just about guaranteed to never get AIDS. Because the HIV germ is not in either of their bodies, they can be very happy together and never infect each other with the HIV virus that will result in AIDS. Do you understand now what AIDS is?

SAM: Thanks, Mom. That helped a lot. But what about condoms? What are they? How do they stop AIDS?

MOM: Well, actually AIDS is the main reason why people are using condoms today. A condom looks a little bit like a balloon, though it is made of something different and tougher than a balloon is. The condom slips over a man's penis before he has sex so that his semen and the skin of his penis cannot touch the other person's body. This helps to protect both of the people who are having sex from catching HIV from each other. The semen is supposed to stay inside the condom, and so hopefully the woman will not get the HIV virus from the man's semen. Using a condom also helps keep a woman from getting pregnant when she has sex, because the sperm in the man's semen is caught in the end of the condom and doesn't get into her vagina and uterus. That is, it doesn't if the condom has been used correctly and doesn't break.

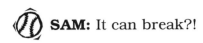 **SAM:** It can break?!

MOM: Many kids think that if they have sex wearing a condom, they are having "safe sex." And they think that as long as sex is safe, it is okay. They are wrong on both points. First, even if sex is safe, it's still wrong if the two people are not married. Even if no one gets pregnant or a disease from having sex, it's still wrong because it isn't what God wants and it isn't what God made sex for. Second, sex is never "safe." People who use condoms do not get pregnant as much as people who don't, and people who use condoms do not get diseases like HIV as much as people who don't. But they still get pregnant sometimes and they still get diseases sometimes because people don't use condoms correctly. Condoms also break fairly often, and the HIV virus is small enough to possibly get through tiny tears in condoms that people cannot see with their eyes. So, sex is never completely safe.

I think God must be really sad when He thinks about people dying of AIDS. God made sex to be a wonderful gift between a wife and her husband. People have so messed up this gift that sex now becomes the way that people infect each other with a disease that can kill them. If people simply followed God's rules about sex, they wouldn't have to be afraid of AIDS.

Some Questions to Discuss

1. Is there such a thing as "safe sex"?
2. How can you be sure of never getting AIDS from sexual intercourse?
3. How should we treat people who have AIDS?

CHAPTER EIGHT

WHAT DOES GAY MEAN?

▼

AMY: Dad, what do they mean when they call a person "gay"? A boy at school said that his uncle is gay. Some of the kids giggled about it. But I don't know what it means.

DAD: This is sort of hard to explain. But I'll do my best, and you can ask any questions you want.

Gay is a word that some people use to describe a man who is homosexual. A woman who is a homosexual is called a lesbian. Some people use the word *gay* to describe both men and women homosexuals.

Now let me tell you what a homosexual is. You know how natural it seems that your mom and I love each other? Because we love each other, we like to kiss and hold each other and be just as close as we can be. We feel strong feelings of love for each other. There are many families, like those in our church, where God has brought together a man and a woman who love each other and want to spend their lives together. God made us so that it is very natural for a man to fall in love with a woman and a woman to fall in love with a man. When you love somebody in that special way as an adult, it is natural to want to hug and kiss and even have sex with the person that you are attracted to. Most people are only attracted to and fall in love with people of the opposite sex—men with women and women with men.

But just because it is natural doesn't mean that it always happens that way. Homosexuals are people who find that they fall in love with and want to kiss, hold, and have sex with people of the same gender (or sex). For example, a gay man is a man who has sex with another man, but not with women. A lesbian is a woman who has sex with another woman, but not with a man.

AMY: But wait a minute! You told me that having sex meant that a man's penis goes into a woman's vagina. How can a man have sex with another man when neither of them has a vagina? And, how can a woman have sex with another woman when neither of them has a penis?

DAD: That is a great question, but I can't give you a whole answer because it is too complicated for you at your age. The basic answer is that they cannot have sexual intercourse the way a husband and wife do, and so they touch each other and hold each other so that they feel good. And some of them say that this is just as good as sexual intercourse for them.

AMY: But are gay people bad? I have heard people in our church talk about gay people as if they are really bad. Are they?

DAD: Well, that depends on what you mean by really bad. Your mom and I believe that the Bible teaches that all of us have bad in us. Romans 3:23 says that "all have sinned and fall short of the glory of God." Everyone has sinned. That means you and I are just as much of a sinner as any homosexual person. And it would certainly not be right to say that all homosexual persons are bad people. When we say that someone is a bad person, we often mean that the person does bad things all the time, that the person enjoys being really evil and never misses an opportunity to do something that is wrong. But all homosexual people are not this way any more than all husbands or wives are this way. Many homosexual people are kind, or hardworking, or truthful, or show other good ways of behaving.

It is still true, though, that God does not want people to do what homosexuals do. The Bible doesn't talk a lot about people acting like homosexuals. But in those few places where it does, the Bible describes it as something wrong that God does not want people to do. For example, Leviticus 18:22 says, "You shall not lie with a male as with a woman; it is an abomination." Clearly, this is something God does not want us to do.

And 1 Corinthians 6:9-11 says, "Do you not know that wrongdoers will not inherit the kingdom of God? Do not be deceived! Fornicators, idolaters, adulterers, male prostitutes, sodomites, thieves, the greedy, drunkards, revilers, robbers—none of these will inherit the kingdom of God." The word *sodomites* is an old-fashioned word for people who engage in homosexual acts. This does not mean that any person who does these things can never get to Heaven. As I understand it, this means that we show who we love by what we do, and people who always break God's rules by continuing to do things God says not to do, those people are showing in their actions that they don't really love God or accept Jesus as their Lord and Savior. That is why your mom and I think that it is a bad choice for people to live that way.

The Bible teaches that God meant for us to fall in love with, marry, and have sex with a person different from us— a woman with a man and a man with a woman. That way we can have children. That way we can show the world in our marriages what His love is like. If we don't get married, for whatever the reason, God wants us to not have sex but to remain a virgin, a person who has never had sex.

 AMY: But why would people do that then? Why would they be homosexual?

DAD: That may be the hardest question of all. Maybe you are really asking two questions: Why do people feel that way? And why do people act that way?

Why do people feel that way? It seems like most homosexual people don't just choose to feel that way. They mostly say they grew up feeling like a homosexual even though they didn't want to. No one knows for sure why some people feel this way when they are adults.

I think the most important thing is for you not to worry about feeling that way. One thing that bothers me about all the talk these days about homosexuals is that some kids worry needlessly about whether they will become homosexual. Not very many people are homosexual; most scientists who study this problem today say that only about two percent, only two people out of every one hundred, are homosexual. When you are growing up and becoming a young man or a young woman, you will have lots of feelings that are hard to explain and that you are not very comfortable with. An awful lot of people who wind up feeling the normal feelings for a husband or a wife have some feelings that seem like homosexual feelings when they are teenagers. I think you don't really need to worry about any troubling feelings you might have in your teenage years, but I would ask you to come talk with me about anything that worries you. It can help just to talk about it, if you

want to; maybe I can help you figure out what your feelings mean. Most of us have to go through a rocky period when we're young. It feels like our bodies and our emotions don't make sense, but we must go through it so that we can grow into the adult God wants us to be.

Why do homosexual people act the way they do? Even if they feel attraction to another homosexual person, why do they live as a homosexual person? Well, not all do. There are Christian men and women who feel those feelings and choose to obey God by not having sex at all. This is the way God wants all people who are not married to behave. And there are some people who acted homosexual for a while, and then God healed them so that they could have a normal marriage.

But there are many homosexuals who act as homosexuals, who "live the gay lifestyle." God does not want this, but they do it anyway. Some do it because they do not believe in God or His rules, and they think that if sex is only for pleasure they can have sex with anyone they want. Some believe in God but believe that the Bible is wrong in what it teaches about how they should act. Some do it because they need someone to love, and the only person or people they can find to love are other homosexuals. Some do it because their lives are very empty and sex is the only joy or reason to live that they can find. And there are many other reasons.

You and I need to remember that God loves homosexual people. Jesus died for them just as He died for you and me. We do not agree with what they are doing; God says it is wrong to live as a homosexual. But they should be treated like all other people.

Some Questions to Discuss
1. What is a homosexual?
2. What does the Bible say about two men or two women having sex together?

CHAPTER NINE

GOD'S RESPONSE TO WRONG

▼

SAM: Mom, what does God think about all the people who break His rules? Does God get really mad at them? Does He hate them?

MOM: That is such a good question. It shows how much you're thinking about the things we're trying to teach you.

You know how when you do something bad, I sometimes get angry at you? Like when I've told you several times not to horse around at the table, but you do it again and spill your drink all over the table? I get really furious. But even when I'm angry, do you think I stop loving you?

SAM: Well, no, but when you're angry I don't feel so loved.

MOM: That's a good, honest answer. It may not show so much then, but even when I'm angry I never stop loving you. God's love is much greater than ours, and He never stops loving us. The Bible says, "For God so loved the world that he gave his only Son, so that everyone who believes in him may not perish but may have eternal life" (John 3:16).

But it is still true that God gets angry when we sin. The Bible is full of verses that show us how angry God gets when we disobey Him. No matter how angry God gets with us, God is always ready to forgive us for the sins that we do. That's why Jesus died on the cross for us. Because God is perfectly fair, He needs to punish us for the wrong that we do. But because He loves us so much, He gave His own Son, Jesus, to the world. Jesus let Himself be punished for all our sins so that we wouldn't have to be punished by God.

And so God is always ready to forgive anyone who comes to Him and sincerely asks to be forgiven. God is always ready to forgive people who misuse His gift of sexuality.

But just because God will forgive us doesn't mean that we are free to break His rules. We all need to decide who it is we really love, who we are really serving. Jesus said, "If you love me, you will keep my commandments" (John 14:15). So people who disobey Jesus' commands and break God's rules over and over again are showing in their actions that they don't really love God. This is why the decisions we make are so important, because we show what is really in our hearts.

When people break God's rules, like when a woman has sex with a man she is not married to or when a man has sex with another man, it makes God very angry and sad to see His marvelous gift of sexuality treated so poorly. But God never stops loving those people. God always calls them to make new and better decisions with their lives. God invites them to be forgiven.

There is one more thing I need to tell you about how God deals with people who break His laws. When people do something that God hates, God is always willing to forgive them for what they have done. But forgiveness doesn't magically correct whatever has gone wrong because of our wrong choices. When you knock over your drink at dinner and I forgive you, the juice doesn't magically jump back off the table and chairs and go back into your glass. The same thing is true about sex.

There are many bad things that can happen because people have sex with each other. Sex outside of marriage is wrong because God tells us not to do it, and we ought to obey Him. Sex outside of marriage is wrong because God made sex as a gift to bond a husband and wife together for life, and it is wrong to use that gift in any other way. But having sex outside of marriage is also wrong because of the terribly bad things that can happen as a result. And God's forgiveness does not make these bad things disappear.

SAM: Like AIDS? When people who disobey God's rules might get AIDS?

MOM: That's right. And while God will always forgive those persons for their sins if they really come to Him with a broken heart and ask for forgiveness, God doesn't usually heal their disease. I don't know if I've said this before, but AIDS is only one of the diseases people catch from having sex outside of marriage. It's the worst, but it isn't the only one.

SAM: Do people ever get pregnant when they aren't married? That happened to a girl in our church, didn't it?

MOM: Right! Yes, anyone who has sex, married or not, can get pregnant. Let's think about pregnancy for a girl. If a fifteen-year-old girl has sex, she is taking a chance on getting pregnant. She may feel bad about what she did in having sex and may pray to God for forgiveness. I believe God will forgive her if she sincerely asks for that forgiveness, but she still may be pregnant. If she is pregnant, a doctor or counselor might suggest she think about getting an abortion. Almost half a million teenage girls a year get abortions. A doctor kills the tiny baby inside her because the girl has decided that a pregnancy and having a baby is not a good thing for her right then. So the first decision she might have to face is whether to get an abortion.

Your father and I believe this is wrong. A woman who has an abortion doesn't have to go through the pregnancy, but she has to live for the rest of her life with the knowledge of what she did to her own son or daughter that she was carrying inside her.

If she decides not to have an abortion, she will have the baby after nine months. Think of what this involves. She will probably have to drop out of school. She will have to go through watching her body change, grow larger, and give birth to a child, probably without a husband around to help. She will find it very difficult to go back to school after having a baby, because babies demand so much care and attention. She will desperately need money to take care of herself, but will have a hard time getting a job because of the care that the baby needs and because she doesn't have a good education. She will need to care for that child for longer than she has been alive herself, for the next eighteen years. She will not fit in with her old friends anymore because they don't have children and can hardly understand why she can't go and do the things that she used to do.

We can also think about it from the boy's perspective. Neither the boy nor the girl usually intends for her to get pregnant, but there is always a chance of that happening. If he gets her pregnant, then he may have to participate in the decision of whether or not to have an abortion.

What if he doesn't believe in abortion, but she gets one anyway? If she chooses not to have an abortion, he has to go through the whole decision about whether the two of them should marry or not. Marriages that start off because of a girl's pregnancy in the teenage years often are not very good marriages. Whether he marries her or not, he ought to participate in supporting the child that is born because of his having sex with the mother. This can result in a young man dropping out of high school and changing his life forever as well, even if he never marries the mother.

 SAM: That sounds awful!

 MOM: It is! It can be very hard on both the young mother and father.

But I think you originally asked me if God hates the people who break His rules. The answer to that question is no. God never stops loving His children, even though their disobedience makes Him very angry. But God does hate the bad things we do. We can be forgiven for the bad things we do, but our lives may be changed forever by the consequences of what we do. Even then, God can bring good out of the worst consequences, like when a person with AIDS becomes a Christian and spends the last months of his or her life loving God and serving Him.

I pray that you will make choices that give God joy. You are in the process of becoming an adult. That means that more and more of your choices will be really big ones that can change your life forever. Of course, your choices matter now. If you spend all of fourth grade goofing off, you will have a harder time in fifth grade, and then you may not do as well in middle school. In the years ahead, you will make decisions about things that could totally change your life forever. For example, by drinking alcohol and driving when you are sixteen, you could get in an accident

and be paralyzed for the rest of your life. Or by deciding to have sex before you are married, you could really hurt yourself and others. Part of growing up is realizing just how big many of the decisions you make really are.

Some Questions to Discuss
1. How can we know that God never stops loving us?
2. How can we express our love for God?
3. Does God's forgiveness take away the bad things that can happen when we make wrong, sinful choices?

CHAPTER TEN

WHAT IS A PERIOD?

▼

AMY: Mom, what is a period? One of my friends said her older sister had started her period. She acted like it was really gross, but I didn't ask her what it meant. What is it?

MOM: Remember how a new person is created when the sperm from a man joins with the egg from a woman inside of her body? The man's sperm gets inside the woman's body when they have sexual intercourse. What I haven't explained to you is how the baby lives inside the mother's body.

AMY: But Mom, what does that have to do with a period?

MOM: You'll see. The growing baby inside the woman's uterus draws all of its air, food, and water directly from its mother's blood. To be able to feed a baby that starts off as tiny as a grain of sand but winds up weighing more than six or seven pounds, the mother needs to have an extra rich supply of blood in her uterus. A woman's body is made so that every month when she might get pregnant, the woman's uterus begins to build up an extra special layer of blood vessels and cells just in case the woman's egg has joined with a sperm to form a tiny baby.

The woman's body is so amazingly sensitive that it usually knows within a few days after a sperm and an egg unite that she is pregnant. Her body knows long before doctors or even the woman herself can tell. Just before her egg is released, her uterus begins to build up this extra layer of blood vessels and cells and blood to get ready in case she gets pregnant. If the sperm and egg unite, so that she is pregnant, her uterus continues to be richly supplied with blood that feeds the baby until it is born many months later. But if she is not pregnant, this extra supply of cells and blood vessels is not needed to nourish the baby. It begins to break up, and suddenly begins to flow out of the woman's body. And this is what is called her menstrual period.

I know I have made it sound like a big event, but it's not really. The uterus is usually small, only about the size of a small apple, so the amount of blood that a woman bleeds is not very much—only about four to six tablespoons over the whole three or four or five days her period lasts.

 AMY: Does it hurt?

MOM: For some women there is no difference at all between the way they feel when they are going through their menstrual period and the way they feel at other times. Others may feel a little discomfort in their stomach area around their uterus or more tired or headachy. Any of these feelings are normal and nothing to worry about.

 AMY: I don't know, Mom. I don't think I'm going to like having a period.

 MOM: I remember feeling just that way. It can be a little awkward and embarrassing at first, but it just takes some getting used to and then it's no big deal. There is nothing unhealthy or dirty about having your period. You simply have to learn to not let the little bit of blood get on your clothes and how to stay clean.

AMY: How do you keep the blood off your clothes?

MOM: There are two things we women use to do this. One is called a sanitary napkin. It's just a thin pad of a cottony paper that you wear in your panties between your legs. The napkin soaks up the little bit of blood and keeps you clean. The other way to stay clean is to use a tampon. A tampon is made of the same kind of stuff as the napkin, except it is packed tighter in a shape like a small tube the size of a short pencil, only about two inches long. A woman pushes the tampon gently into her vagina, and it soaks in the blood from her period there inside her vagina. The packages of sanitary napkins and tampons contain careful instructions for how to use them. A girl must never try to push anything up into her vagina except a tampon, and we should talk about it before you try so that I can answer any questions you might have. Most girls use sanitary napkins rather than tampons.

Having a menstrual period is a marvelous thing. It is a sign that the woman can get pregnant. It is a sign of how wonderfully God has made her body to carry life within it.

Some Questions to Discuss

1. What are some things you have heard about how girls start having their periods and what it is like for them?

2. How do you feel about someday starting your period?

CHAPTER ELEVEN

WHAT IS SEXUAL ABUSE?

▼

 DAD: Kids, I want to talk to you both about what we call "sexual abuse." Have you ever heard that term?

 SAM: I think so, Dad, but I'm not sure what it means.

DAD: Well, I want to talk to you both about this subject because it is so much in the news these days. Do you remember yesterday when we had the TV news on while we were putting dinner on the table? The reporter talked about a teacher who had sexually abused some children. I thought it would be good for us to talk about the subject.

 AMY: Well, what did that mean, Dad?

 DAD: The phrase "sexual abuse" refers to an adult or older kid, like a teenager, using a child's body for the adult's or older kid's sexual pleasure. We talked before about how God made our bodies and our sexuality for us to enjoy but that God means for marriage to be the only place where we experience sexual intercourse. This is why God set up His rule that two people should not have sex unless they are married. God hopes this rule will protect us against misusing the marvelous gift that He gave us by making our bodies. People break these rules in all sorts of ways and for all sorts of reasons. People break God's rules when someone who is married has sex with someone other than his or her husband or wife. People break the rules when they have sex before they get married.

 MOM: And one of the ways people break God's rules is through sexual abuse. People do what we call sexual abuse for a lot of different reasons. People who hate God and want to do what is bad instead of good will sometimes look at God's rules and then try to do the worst possible things they can to break those rules. So it is possible that some people who engage in sexual abuse do so because of evil that is in their hearts.

Some people do it because of horrible things that happened to them when they were growing up; maybe they were sexually abused themselves. These sorts of things can really twist people's hearts and minds so that it feels more natural to them to be sexually interested in a child than someone else. Other people might be so lonely or depressed or confused that they sexually abuse a child as a way to forget their unhappiness. There are probably other reasons as well.

 AMY: But, Mom, what is sexual abuse?

 MOM: I hate even talking about it, because the very thought of it makes me upset, sad, and angry at the same time. But it is important to talk about, because I want to protect you and teach you to protect yourself.

Sexual abuse can happen to kids of all ages. It can happen to a baby or a child who is only two or three. It can happen to a sixteen- or seventeen-year-old girl or boy.

Sexual abuse can happen when a grownup or even an older child kisses or touches a younger child, like if an older kid forced you to kiss him, or an adult put his hand between your legs to touch your privates. Another type of sexual abuse can be when an adult or older child forces a child to touch his genitals or other parts of his body in a sexual way. Or sexual abuse can be when a person shows his sexual organs—his private parts—to the child, or even if he shows the child pictures of naked people. That's what we call pornography. And sometimes it can mean the adult actually having sexual intercourse with the child.

 SAM: That's gross!

 DAD: It's gross and it is evil, Sam. We don't want to frighten you by telling you this. Thankfully, sexual abuse doesn't happen that often. But it is said that there are a fair number of people who have experienced sexual abuse in their life. The people who commit acts of sexual abuse are almost always men. Most of the time, girls are the ones who are abused, but sexual abuse is also directed at boys sometimes. That's why we wanted to talk to both of you.

AMY: But what are you supposed to do about it? How do you keep it from happening?

DAD: I'm really glad you asked that question, because that is exactly what I was going to talk about next. I want you to understand that not everything that is unpleasant is sexual abuse. Remember years ago when you were little and you came in crying because the little boy up the street pulled his underwear down and wiggled his rear end at you? That was rude, but it wasn't really sexual abuse. And you remember how at the last family reunion Great Aunt Liddy, bless her soul, grabbed your little sister and smothered her with kisses even though she was fighting to get away? Well, that wasn't sexual abuse either.

 SAM: Then how can you tell what is sexual abuse?

 MOM: There are three important things that I would like you to remember.

First, remember that it is an absolute rule that no one has the right to see the private parts of your body—the genital area for boys and the breasts and the genital area for girls—except a doctor who is examining you and your parents under certain circumstances, like if you are hurt or something. No one has a right to touch you there either. If anyone tries to make you do either of those things—to see and touch you or to have you see and touch that person—you should immediately try to get out of the situation and tell us right away so that we can help you decide what to do. It is our job as parents to protect you.

The second rule is that you should trust your feelings about what you like and feel comfortable with and what you don't like and don't feel comfortable with. For instance, suppose one of your friends had a real "kissy" family, and after a while someone in that family gave you a kiss. A little kiss itself is not sexual abuse, but if that kiss isn't comfortable for you, and if we talk about it and we're not comfortable about it either, then it is like sexual abuse if that person keeps doing it after we ask him or her to stop.

The third thing is that you should not keep secrets

about these kinds of things. If anything ever happens that makes you feel uncomfortable, you should tell us right away. We are here to protect you, but we can only protect you if we know what is going on.

It is very important for you to know that you can protect yourself against sexual abuse. The best thing is to be very strong and confident that you know what is right and wrong. Also, you must know that you will get our help in dealing with anything bad that happens to you. If anyone ever tries to kiss you or touch you or get you to do something that you are not completely sure is right, you should speak very strongly and say, "I am not going to do that, and I am going to talk to my mother and father about this." If anyone ever begs you not to tell us or even threatens you, don't you believe what they say; they are lying. Sometimes sexual abusers make up stories about how they belong to the police and that if a child tells his or her mom and dad the police will get the mother and father in trouble. They may even threaten to hurt the mother and father. Don't you believe it if someone says something like that. They are only lying to scare you and get what they want. We as your mom and dad can protect ourselves, and we can protect you. So no secrets like that—never!

AMY: But how do kids feel if something like that has happened to them? What happens to children that sexual abuse happens to?

MOM: Sexual abuse can make the child very sad and very upset for a long time. The most important thing is for the child to talk with his or her mother and father about it so that they can help decide what is best to do. Sometimes it helps a child to talk to a doctor or counselor about what happened. It may be very important for the people who did the sexual abuse to get arrested and go to jail as a way of punishing them and stopping them from hurting anybody else.

Another important thing is for a child to realize that it was not her or his fault. People who do such abuse try to make the child feel like it was the child's fault. This is never true! It is never a child's fault when something like this happens.

DAD: Some older children commit sexual abuse because they themselves have been sexually abused. We know one family where the son was sexually abused when he was four. He was sexually abused by a seven-year-old neighbor. The seven-year-old had been shown very dirty, evil movies by an adult and had probably done some of the things that were shown in those movies with the adult. So this seven-year-old boy had terribly wrong ideas about sex and what he should do with his body. Then he carried out those ideas with the four-year-old. That seven-year-old boy needed help, and the grownup who got him into that kind of behavior needed to be punished and helped.

We really want you two to be able to protect yourselves against sexual abuse, and we want you to be able to come to us for protection. If you can remember anything like this ever happening to you, we want to talk with you about it, because it was not your fault and it is not something that needs to be a secret. Often, things that we keep secret have a terrible effect on us. But when we talk about them, God can help us heal from what happened.

MOM: We've talked a lot about bad things that can happen. But remember that our sexuality is a wonderful and beautiful gift from God. Sexual abuse is an evil way that people use a wonderful gift to do wrong. My hope is that you can be protected from this because we have talked openly about it, and I certainly want to work hard to protect you. I want to help protect you so that you can go on to have a life where you honor God by the way that you handle being a man and a woman.

Some Questions to Discuss
1. What is sexual abuse?
2. Should you ever keep a secret about someone trying to touch you or abuse you?

CHAPTER TWELVE

GROWING UP

▼

AMY: Mom and Dad, I've been thinking about some of the stuff we've been talking with you guys about. About sex and stuff. I don't know if I can say it right, but I guess I'm not sure I want to grow up. I mean, you say sex is a wonderful gift and all that, but it seems like there are some things to be scared about when you're a grownup. I'm not sure I'm ready for that.

SAM: I feel that way, too! I'd like to be married some-day and all that, but it doesn't sound as easy or as fun as I thought it would be.

MOM: I think I understand just what you mean. You aren't ready to handle some of these things yet, and that makes them sound really scary. The reason we are talking about them with you now is to help you be ready when it is time for you to make decisions, like when there's a boy or girl you really like when you are

sixteen. Everyone, even grownups, is a bit scared of handling situations and making decisions that he or she has never faced before. By talking about it ahead of time, we help get ready to make those decisions. Did you know your dad and I were excited but scared about having kids? Talking about what it would be like to have kids and how we might handle some tough situations really helped us get ready to be parents.

DAD: I agree. Also, as we live in our family and have our nice friends and go to church, it can seem like everything happens so easily and naturally. But the world is a scary place, even for us adults. I don't like it that there are so many problems for people to face, even the people we love—problems like diseases and unwanted pregnancies. I hate it that so many people disagree about important things, like whether it is a good thing to have sex before you are married with someone you are just dating.

That's why we must have courage. Courage is when we have the strength to do what is right even when we're nervous or scared. God can give us that courage. If we trust God, believe that He tells us the truth in the Bible, and ask Him to forgive us and help us do what is right, we believe God will answer that prayer. He will give us the courage and the strength to do what is right. I wish being a Christian was easy, but it never has been easy. And many Christians have had to face a much more difficult world than we do!

AMY: But is it worth it to grow up? With all the problems and all?

DAD: Yes, it is, Amy. I had a wonderful childhood, filled with a lot of joy. I hope your childhood is even better. Some other people aren't as fortunate and look back on many difficult times in childhood. But even so, the joys of being an adult are special. The hard parts about being an adult actually make the good things that much more wonderful.

And sexuality is part of that. My love for Christ is the most important thing in my life. But next to God, I love your mother and you kids the most. You guys make my life full of joy! And without sexuality, there would be no marriage, no children, no families. I'm glad you love being a child, but in a few more years you will begin to feel ready to move on to becoming an adult; you'll be ready to trade in the joys of childhood for the deeper and more complicated joys of adulthood.

MOM: And when you are ready, I hope that having talked about sex in our family will help you make right decisions. One of the wonderful things about the Christian faith is that we can trust that God helps us with the toughest decisions of our lives, by showing us the right way in the Bible, the way He wants us to live.

But another wonderful thing about the Christian faith is that our God never stops loving us, even when we make wrong decisions. He can forgive us for what we did wrong and help us rebuild our lives. It's better to make the right decision in the first place, because then we don't have as much painful rebuilding to do! But isn't it wonderful that our Lord is so full of forgiveness and truth?

SAM: And I guess there's nothing we can do about it anyway. We can't stay kids.

MOM: That's right! So enjoy being kids! And talk with us about anything that you wonder about or that bothers you. It is a joy, a privilege, to talk with you guys about these things. We are always ready to talk and pray with you.

Some Questions to Discuss
1. How do you feel about growing up—excited, scared, confident, or what?
2. How does talking to your mom or dad about sex feel to you?

AUTHORS

Stanton L. Jones, Ph.D., is professor and chairperson of the Department of Psychology at Wheaton College, where he has been directing the development of the college's doctoral program in clinical psychology. He coauthored *Modern Psychotherapies: A Comprehensive Christian Appraisal* with Richard E. Butman, and edited *Psychology and the Christian Faith: An Introductory Reader*. He has contributed a number of articles to professional journals and to magazines such as *Christianity Today*.

Brenna B. Jones is a mother whose goals have focused on the nurture and formation of the character of her children. Her undergraduate studies were in landscape architecture at Texas A & M University. She has served as a leader in a Bible study ministry with women for a number of years.

Brenna and Stan are active in a church ministry to engaged couples. They make their home in Wheaton, Illinios, where they parent three children: Jenny, Brandon, and Lindsay.